WEAPONS AND MACHINES IN WARFARE

I0804455

WEAPONS AND MACHINES OF WORLD WAR I

Craig Boutland

Cavendish Square

Published in 2024 by Cavendish Square Publishing, LLC
2544 Clinton Street, Buffalo, NY 14224

Copyright © 2023 Brown Bear Books Ltd.

Portions of this work were originally authored by Charlie Samuels and published as *Machines and Weaponry of World War I*. All new material this edition authored by Craig Boutland.

No part of this publication may be reproduced, stored in a retrieval system, or transmitted in any form or by any means—electronic, mechanical, photocopying, recording, or otherwise—without the prior permission of the copyright owner. Request for permission should be addressed to Permissions, Cavendish Square Publishing, 2544 Clinton Street, Buffalo, NY 14224. Tel (877) 980-4450; fax (877) 980-4454.

Website: cavendishsq.com

This publication represents the opinions and views of the author based on his or her personal experience, knowledge, and research. The information in this book serves as a general guide only. The author and publisher have used their best efforts in preparing this book and disclaim liability rising directly or indirectly from the use and application of this book.

All websites were available and accurate when this book was sent to press.

Design Manager: Keith Davis
Picture Manager: Sophie Mortimer

Picture Credits
Front Cover: Robert Hunt Library
All photographs Robert Hunt Library Except: adamsguns.com: 32bl; Jean-Louis Dubois: 24br; Hmaag: 33; Library of Congress: 32r, 37tr; NJR ZA: 7tr; Shutterstock: Chris Alcock 20, Mac1 1, 18, 44, Charles F. McCarthy 35b, Sura M. Naulpradid 13br; Thinkstock: iStockphoto 16r, Photos.com 29; U.S. Army: 24l; John Woolford: 10, 34, 40.
Key: t = top, c = center, b = bottom, l = left, r = right.

Cataloging-in-Publication Data

Names: Boutland, Craig.
Title: Weapons and machines of World War I / Craig Boutland.
Description: Buffalo, New York : Cavendish Square Publishing, 2024. | Series: Weapons and machines in warfare | Includes glossary and index.
Identifiers: ISBN 9781502669230 (pbk.) | ISBN 9781502669247 (library bound) | ISBN 9781502669254 (ebook)
Subjects: LCSH: World War, 1914-1918--Equipment and supplies--Juvenile literature. | Military weapons--History--20th century--Juvenile literature. | World War, 1914-1918--United States--Juvenile literature.
Classification: LCC D522.7 B66 2024 | DDC 940.4'83--dc23

CPSIA compliance information: Batch #CSCSQ24: For further information contact Cavendish Square Publishing LLC at 1-877-980-4450.

Printed in the United States of America

Find us on

CONTENTS

Introduction

The countries that took part in World War I (1914–1918) had advanced industries and could develop powerful new technologies. For the first time, aircraft were a major weapon, and warfare took to the skies. Artillery pieces became huge, and shells and bombs could now hit targets from farther ranges than ever before. On battlefields, soldiers faced threats from rapid-firing machine guns and poison gas.

Czech soldiers man an armored train late in the war. Armored trains were unusual, but they demonstrated how all sides tried to make the most of technology to help the war effort.

artillery: Cannons and other big guns that fire large shells over long distances.

British shells explode near a line of German battleships in the Battle of Jutland in June 1916. The battle was one of the few large-scale engagements between the British and German fleets during the war.

The war was fought on many fronts. Germany and its allies fought Britain and France in the west and the Russian Empire in the east. There was fighting in European colonies in Africa and Asia. In 1917, the United States joined the Allied side after a German submarine sank a liner carrying U.S. passengers.

TRENCH WARFARE

On the Western Front, the war became largely static by the end of 1914. The two sides faced each other in lines of **trenches**, often so close soldiers could shout to one another. Many of the developments in weapons technology during the war were a reaction to this new form of warfare.

trenches: Defensive positions that were dug into the ground.

18-pounder

Artillery killed more men than machine-gun bullets did during World War I. The main artillery gun of Great Britain and its empire was the Ordnance QF 18-pounder. The gun got its name from the weight of its shells: 18½ pounds (8.4 kg). These guns fired about 99,397,670 rounds on the Western Front alone, but the 18-pounder was used on every other front as well. It remained in use until 1942.

A **battery** of 18-pounders in the field. The guns were used to create "rolling barrages," behind which the infantry advanced as the shelling moved forward.

battery: A group of artillery weapons that operate together as one unit.

More than 12,000 18-pounders were produced during the war. The gun was used everywhere that British or Commonwealth forces fought.

NEW TECHNOLOGY

First produced in 1904, the 18-pounder was still a relatively new technology in 1914. Its barrel had been modified to make it more reliable. The gun's large wheels helped it move across uneven ground.

The quick-firing gun was pulled by six horses on a two-wheeled ammunition limber. The gun had a crew of ten, six of whom actually fired it. Each gun weighed 2,820 lbs (1,279 kg) and could fire high-explosive shells up to 3.7 miles (almost 6 km).

Thousands of used shell casings piled up at a British position on the Western Front.

SHELLSHOCK

British field guns fired four types of shell. **Shrapnel** shells were used to cut barbed wire. High-explosive shells were used against trenches and other defenses. Smoke shells screened troop movements, while gas shells released poison gas on landing. A well-trained crew could fire about 30 rounds per minute. During the summer of 1917, British guns fired 1 million rounds per week.

shrapnel: Fragments of metal that fly out of an exploding shell.

Airship

Balloons and airships were used extensively during World War I. They were used for **reconnaissance**, artillery spotting, and later for air defense of cities. However, they were also used to drop bombs, particularly by the Germans. German cigar-shaped balloons, up to 650 feet (200 m) long, were known as Zeppelins and brought fear to allied cities.

An airship flies overhead as British troops wait in the harbor at Mudros in Greece before the landings at Gallipoli in Turkey in August 1915.

reconnaissance: Gathering information about enemy positions.

The British airship R26 flies over London. The British mainly used airships to protect cities against bombing raids.

THE ZEPPELIN

The airship invented by a German count, Ferdinand von Zeppelin, was intended to cause widespread destruction. However, the first Zeppelin attack on London in May 1915 killed only seven people. After 53 out of 77 Zeppelins were destroyed by enemy fire or bad weather, the Germans abandoned the campaign.

A FORMIDABLE WEAPON

Airships could fly higher than the earliest warplanes. If, by chance, they met an enemy fighter, the airships carried machine guns for defense. They flew their long-range missions at night, so they could not be seen by gunners on the ground.

An airship had a steel skeleton. Its balloon of fabric was inflated with hydrogen. Four engines propelled it at up to 60 miles per hour (100 km/h). It could carry nearly two tons of bombs, far more than any other aircraft. However, once **incendiary** bullets were developed, airships could be blown up easily. After a peak in 1915, airship use became less frequent. It stopped completely in August 1918.

incendiary: Something that is designed to start a fire.

Armored Car

Early in the war, the British adopted an idea from Belgium and fitted **plate armor** to a powerful automobile. This new weapon surprised enemy forces and became even more useful when a revolving turret carrying a gun was added. Armored cars were mobile and effective on firm ground but became bogged down in mud. Their tires were also easily punctured by small arms fire.

British Rolls Royce automobiles were given plate armor and machine guns and used to make raids on the enemy. After trench warfare came to dominate the Western Front, they were used in the Middle East and in Russia.

plate armor: Armor made from flat sheets of iron welded or riveted together.

ROLLS ROYCES AT WAR

A British military commander, the Duke of Westminster, suggested the government should seize all Rolls Royce Silver Ghosts (a type of luxury car) in the country. Armored bodywork was added to the car, and a **turret** with a machine gun was fitted.

ARAB HERO

The British officer T.E. Lawrence—"Lawrence of Arabia"—coordinated the Arab revolt against the Ottoman Empire in 1916. He called his unit of nine armored Rolls Royces "more valuable than rubies." The cars took part in raids to blow up bridges and rip up railroad tracks, as well as helping to seize 200 rifles and 80,000 rounds of ammunition.

The duke took his Rolls Royces first to France and then to Egypt to rescue prisoners of war in the Sahara Desert in 1915–1916. His Light Armored Car Brigade—with nine armored cars—captured enemy guns at Bir Assis. Later in 1916 and 1917, armored cars were used again in the desert to repel the enemy.

Armored cars move forward at Biefvillers on the Western Front.

A Rolls Royce armored car comes under shellfire in open land on the Eastern Front.

turret: A revolving structure placed on top of a vehicle or ship, usually to house a gun.

Barbed Wire

Barbed wire had originally been used as fencing on farms. It was wire that had sharp points, or "barbs," along its length, so it was painful for animals if they tried to get through it. On the Western Front, wire was laid in great coils to trap enemy soldiers moving forward. When they slowed to get through the wire, they became targets for the machine guns and artillery of the defending force.

A shell bursts in **no-man's land** beyond barbed wire guarding British positions. Laying the wire was dangerous work, often undertaken at night.

no-man's land: The land lying between the enemy trench lines on the Western Front.

British troops take cover behind a barbed-wire barrier during the Battle of the Lys in Belgium in 1918.

WIRE DANGERS

Setting up barbed wire in no-man's land was a dangerous job. The wire was always set away from the trenches so that the enemy could not get close enough to throw **grenades**.

Barbed wire was almost impossible to pass through. Wire cutters could cut it, but that was another risky job. Heavy shelling was sometimes used to blow it up, but often it just threw the barbed wire in the air and created a bigger tangle than before. Getting caught on the wire was horrible; soldiers who could not be rescued died a slow and painful death being shot at by the enemy.

EYEWITNESS

"One night we heard a cry...then all was quiet again...[A]n hour later the cry came again. It never ceased the whole night. Nor the following night...Later we learned that it was one of our own men hanging on the wire. Nobody could do anything for him."

Ernst Toller
Infantryman, German Army

grenade: A small bomb that can be thrown by an infantryman.

Battleship

During the 19th century, Britain was the world's leading naval power. In 1906, it built HMS *Dreadnought*. This was the most powerful battleship then known, with huge guns, heavy armor, and steam-driven engines. Similar battleships were called dreadnoughts. The Germans began building their own massive battleships. By 1914, Britain had 21 dreadnoughts and Germany had 13.

A line of British dreadnoughts fires a **broadside** toward the German fleet at the Battle of Jutland in 1916.

broadside: When all the guns on one side of a ship fire at the same time.

When HMS *Dreadnought* was built in 1906, it started a race between Britain and Germany to build powerful new battleships as quickly as possible.

Smoke pours from the funnels of British battleships as they steam in a formation known as line astern, or one after another.

INCONCLUSIVE BATTLE

At the Battle of Jutland in May 1916, the British and German fleets fought a large-scale battle. Britain lost 14 ships, while the Germans lost 11. Neither side lost any dreadnoughts. The losses were mainly among smaller warships—cruisers and destroyers. After Jutland, the German fleet withdrew to port. Britain and France then **blockaded** German trade routes during the winter of 1916–1917. Hungry German citizens had to survive on homegrown turnips.

EYEWITNESS

"There was a terrific explosion aboard the ship. . . I saw the guns go up in the air just like matchsticks—12-inch [30.5 cm] guns they were—bodies and everything. . . Within half a minute the ship turned right over and she was gone."

C. Farmer
Signaler, HMS *Indefatigable*

blockade: To use ships to prevent a country from importing or exporting supplies.

U.S. infantrymen practice attack and defense with bayonets.

Bayonet

The bayonet was a small sword that could be attached to the end of a rifle. It had first been introduced in the 17th century. It was ideal for **close-quarter fighting**, and infantry trained for long periods in using it. However, by the time of World War I, bayonets killed or wounded few troops. Bullets and artillery shells were far more deadly.

close-quarter: Hand-to-hand fighting with an enemy who is within touching distance.

Canadian troops fix bayonets to their rifles shortly before going "**over the top**" in an attack on the enemy lines.

BAYONET

Soldiers were trained to slash at an enemy's "vulnerable points," such as the throat, chest, or groin. In the trenches of the Western Front, however, the bayonet often had to be used to stab rather than slash, as there was no room to swing it.

The German Army used more types of bayonet than the Allies. Overall, however, it made little difference. The importance of the bayonet lay in its power to terrify the enemy rather than in its real power as a weapon.

EYEWITNESS

"A French corporal suddenly stood before me, both our bayonets at the ready, he to kill me, I to kill him... pushing his weapon aside I stabbed him in the chest. He dropped his rifle and fell, and the blood shot out of his mouth."

Stephan Westman
Coroporal, German army

The bayonet was designed primarily as a slashing weapon, rather than for stabbing.

over the top: The name for the moment soldiers left their trenches to begin an advance.

Biplane

In 1914, the airplane was a new technology, and military establishments were still working out how best to use it. Airplanes originally took to the skies to find out about enemy positions. If they got close, the pilots fired at each other with **pistols**. In 1915, aircraft began mounting forward-firing machine guns. Airplanes then began deliberately taking each other on in deadly aerial combat.

The Sopwith Pup was used by the British from 1916 until late 1917, when it was outclassed by new German aircraft.

 pistols: Small handguns often carried by officers, pilots, and other soldiers.

The Sopwith Camel was the most successful Allied fighter of the war. It was credited with shooting down 1,294 enemy aircraft with its twin machine guns.

FIGHTING THE FOKKER

The introduction of a biplane armed with a machine gun marked a new stage of air combat. The British company Vickers produced the first war plane in 1915. By the end of that year, however, German Fokker airplanes controlled the skies.

When the British had a chance to examine a shot-down Fokker, Allied aircraft began to improve. New models were in the air by mid-1916. The Sopwith Camel was one of the best. It could turn sharply and maneuver into a spin. With a good pilot, it could beat the German Fokker on any given day.

INTERRUPTER

Machine guns were mounted on the back of biplanes until 1915. The German Fokker had a forward-facing machine gun that allowed the pilot to fly and fire at the same time. The gun relied on an interrupter invented by Fokker. The device synchronized the gun's firing to stop bullets from hitting the **propeller** blades as they spun.

propeller: The revolving blades that power an airplane through the air.

The French knew the gun as the Soixante-Quinze, or "seventy-five," for the caliber of its shells.

French 75mm

During the 1890s, the French army developed a new piece of artillery that was the best in the world for the time. This was the 75mm field gun. It was lightweight and fired very quickly. It could shoot off 20 rounds a minute, whereas other field guns could manage just six rounds a minute. This was because its **recoil** mechanism meant the gun was instantly ready to fire again. The "75" was the standard French artillery piece of World War I.

recoil: The kickback of a gun when it is fired.

One of the crew loads a shell into a gun while others prepare to pass the gunner more ammunition.

Crew in action early in World War I. The shells were carried in a limber attached to the gun.

THE 75 IN ACTION

The French Army had around 3,800 75s in 1914, compared with just 389 heavy guns. Each gun had a crew of nine men. A team of six horses pulled the gun and its ammunition **limber**.

The gun had limitations. It was not designed for firing at a high angle to drop shells on top of well-made trenches. French commanders actively sought new artillery to use in trench warfare, but the 75mm continued to be used. By the end of World War I, the French had 17,000 in the field.

ON THE MARNE

The 75mm proved its worth at the Battle of the Marne (September 5–12, 1914). Commanded by Marshal Foch, the French halted their retreat and stood to face the advancing Germans. The 75mm was effective in the open countryside. It supported the attacking infantry and stopped the Germans from advancing on Paris.

limber: A two-wheeled vehicle that can carry a gun or a container of ammunition.

U.S. troops on the Western Front watch gas drift toward the German lines. The weapon could be unpredictable, as it depended on the direction of the wind.

Gas

Advances in chemical technology during the late 19th century meant that many lethal gases had been invented. At Ypres on April 22, 1915, German forces released chlorine that the wind then blew toward the enemy. Soldiers who breathed it in would choke and could later die. After that, both the Germans and the allies used gas. It was a terrifying weapon.

chlorine: A chemical that, as a gas, can irritate the lungs and cause suffocation and death.

GAS ATTACK

By 1918, around 25 percent of British shells and 80 percent of German shells carried gas. Both sides used phosgene gas starting in 1916. It killed victims within 24 hours. Dichlorethylsulphide, better known as "mustard gas," was introduced in 1917. It killed more men than any other gas. The victims slowly choked to death. Men were still dying from its effects after the war had ended.

To protect themselves, soldiers first used handkerchiefs soaked in water. Later, hoods and gas masks—face masks with air filters—were developed both for soldiers and for horses.

EYEWITNESS

"Gas! Gas! Quick, boys! – An ecstasy of fumbling,
Fitting the clumsy helmets just in time;
But someone still was yelling out and stumbling,
And flound'ring like a man in fire or lime. . ."

"Dulce et Decorum est,"
by war poet **Wilfred Owen**

German gas drifts toward Allied lines at Halluch in April 1916—one of the most intense gas attacks of the war.

The Livens Projector was a simple type of mortar that was the most common means of launching shells containing poison gas.

Livens Projector: A series of semi-buried tubes that fired mortar charges.

Grenades

The word grenade comes from the Spanish word for "pomegranate" because the first grenades had the same shape as this fruit. Special units called "grenadiers" were formed in the 18th century to throw these small bombs. During World War I, when armies were **dug in**, grenades were useful for tossing into enemy positions. By 1915, the British produced 500,000 grenades a week.

The uneven case of the Mills bomb was intended to shatter and throw as much shrapnel as possible.

This U.S. soldier practices throwing a grenade. The British based their technique on the sport of cricket.

dug in: Protected in strong defensive positions by trenches and other barriers.

French soldiers prepare to throw grenades from their own trench toward enemy positions.

THE MILLS BOMB

There were more than 50 types of grenade, but they all had a metal case filled with explosives, with a **fuse** to ignite them. The most popular British grenade was the Mills bomb. It was activated when the thrower pulled out a safety pin. Four seconds later, the grenade exploded into lots of pieces to cause maximum damage.

Soldiers took lessons in tossing grenades so they could use them at a moment's notice. By the end of the war, the Allies had thrown some 70 million Mills bombs and 35 million other grenades.

EYEWITNESS

"All bombers must be supplied with a left-handed glove or finger stall. We discovered that the men's fingers got absolutely raw from pinching in the split pin and drawing out the ring from the Mills bomb."

Notes from the Front
British Army magazine

fuse: A mechanical or electrical device for detonating the explosives in a bomb.

A British crew prepares to fire a 12-inch (30.5 cm) howitzer. The gun had a range of up to 8 miles (13 km). The gun could be broken into sections and moved on traction engine wheels.

Howitzer

Early in World War I it became clear that artillery needed to fire at targets well behind enemy lines, where the target could not be seen by the gunners. Howitzers were developed to fulfil this need. They fired shells on a high **trajectory** at targets up to 8 miles (13 km) away. The shells traveled more slowly than bullets from field guns but caused great damage when they landed.

trajectory: The path of a flying object from when it is launched until it lands.

BIGGER AND BIGGER

Howitzers were not easy to move. Early in the war, they were taken apart and pulled around by horses. By 1918, they were moved on tractors or railroad cars.

The Germans got a head start, but in 1915 the British produced the 6-inch (15.25 cm) howitzer, followed by 9- and 12-inch (23 and 30.5 cm) versions. It was used before infantry attacks to cut barbed wire and destroy frontline trenches. The importance of the weapon is clear from the number of shells it fired: 22.4 million rounds on the Western Front alone.

BIG BERTHA

Dicke Bertha—"big" or "fat" Bertha—was a super-heavy howitzer used by the German Army. It could fire a 240-lb (110 kg) shell at a target 90 miles (148 km) away. Twelve were made, but only two were available at the start of the war. They were spectacularly successful. They destroyed forts in Belgium and boosted German confidence at the start of the war.

British artillerymen pose with a 12-inch (30.5 cm) howitzer nicknamed "Bunty" at Soissons, France.

The British Vickers 9.2-inch howitzer was the main weapon used by the Allies on the Western Front to counterattack German artillery positions

counterattack: To attack the enemy after they have attacked you.

The barrel of this machine gun is enclosed in a chamber of water to act as a cooler and prevent the gun from overheating.

Machine Gun

Machine guns had first been developed in the late 19th century. During World War I, machine guns could fire an average 600 **rounds** a minute. During the late summer and autumn of 1914, machine guns took a terrible toll on soldiers fighting in the open. Soon, long lines of trenches were dug for protection from the hail of bullets. The machine gun had changed the face of warfare.

round: The military name for a single shot fired by a weapon.

The Vickers machine gun was known as "the Queen of the Battlefield." Gunners loved it because it was so reliable.

LIGHT MACHINE GUNS

With the development of lighter guns like the British **Lewis gun**, crews could carry machine guns with them when they attacked. By 1915, the British were equipped with the Vickers machine gun. The Vickers was completely reliable. In August 1916, British troops fired more than 1 million rounds from Vickers guns in just 12 hours.

The machine gun dominated the battlefield because of the intensity of its fire. In the Battle of the Somme, German machine guns cut down some 60,000 advancing British troops.

EYEWITNESS

"The officers were in the front. I noticed one of them walking calmly carrying a walking stick. When we started firing we just had to load and reload. They went down in their hundreds. You didn't have to aim, we just fired into them."

German machine gunner
Battle of the Somme, 1916

Lewis gun: A light, gas-operated machine gun with a circular drum cartridge.

Mines

Digging under enemy defenses had been used during the Middle Ages to attack castles. It was brought back as a strategy in World War I when the long trench systems of the Western Front led to **stalemate**. Unable to attack in the open, both sides began digging tunnels beneath no-man's land to place bombs under enemy trenches. In the first use of mining on the Western Front, the Germans destroyed a whole brigade of Belgian troops.

A plume of dirt marks the explosion of a mine buried beneath the ground.

stalemate: A point at which neither side can gain an advantage over the other.

HORRIBLE CONDITIONS

Starting in February 1915, the British created tunneling companies of men who were miners in civilian life. Even for them, tunneling was a horrible job. They worked in freezing conditions, often in 1 foot (30.5 cm) of water, for 12 hours at a time. Sometimes enemy tunnelers met and fought underground, using their shovels and picks as weapons.

By early 1917, British and French tunnelers dominated. Their superior listening equipment, such as the **geophone**, gave them a real advantage over the Germans.

MESSINES RIDGE

British miners spent a year in 1916–1917 digging tunnels under Messines Ridge, near Ypres, to place 600 tons (545 t) of explosive beneath the German trenches. The mines were detonated at 3:10 a.m. on June 7, 1917. The explosion was heard in London, Britain, 130 miles (210 km) away. Some 10,000 German soldiers died, and a British advance captured all its objectives.

A mine blows up beneath German lines at the Battle of Messines Ridge in June 1917.

British miners place explosives in a chamber before the start of the Battle of the Somme in 1916.

geophone: A device that detects vibrations passing through rock and earth.

Pistols

Pistols are much less accurate than rifles, but they became important for various types of soldiers during World War I. Officers had traditionally carried pistols and continued to do so after 1914. However, troops who fought in the cramped spaces of tanks were also equipped with pistols, while machine gunners carried pistols because their hands were full with the machine gun and its ammunition.

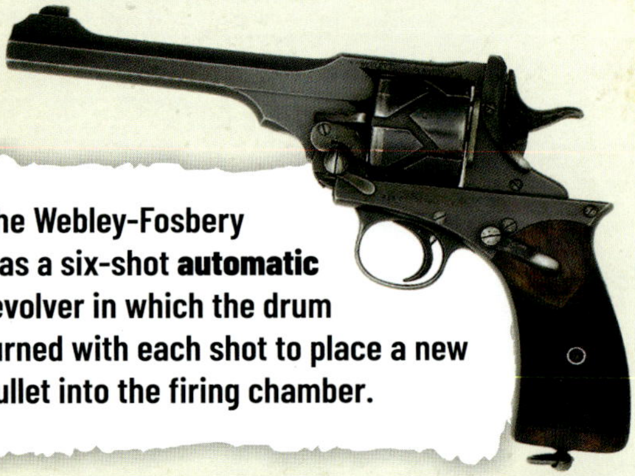

The Webley-Fosbery was a six-shot **automatic** revolver in which the drum turned with each shot to place a new bullet into the firing chamber.

An American Marine officer carries a Colt pistol in this detail from a recruiting poster.

automatic: A weapon that continues to fire until the trigger is released.

TYPES OF PISTOL

There were three types of pistol: revolvers, clip-loaded automatics, and "blow-back" models, which got energy from the gases given off by firing the previous cartridge.

The British used the Webley Mark IV revolver. It required a lot of practice to shoot, however, because it jumped when it was fired. The U.S. Army and Navy used three pistols. They included the popular 1911 model Colt .45 and the Smith and Wesson. Relatively few men died from pistol shots, but the pistol was a vital part of an officer's armory.

LUGER PISTOL

Probably the most famous pistol of the war was the German Luger P08, a 9mm **semiautomatic** handgun. Although more than two million were manufactured, the pistol was always in short supply because its accuracy and reliability meant it was highly sought after. Allied soldiers used captured Lugers in preference to their own weapons.

The 1911 model Colt was one of the most popular Allied handguns.

semiautomatic: A weapon that can fire repeatedly, but only if the trigger is pressed each time.

Renault FT Tank

In 1916, tanks became one of the key weapons used on the Western Front. Heavy tanks could break into defenses, but it became clear that a lighter, more maneuverable tank was needed to rush through any gap. The French answer was the Renault FT **light tank**. Many experts describe it as the first modern tank. Although it was not very fast by modern standards, it had revolutionary new features.

The Renault had a top speed of 4.3 miles per hour (7 km/h). It was intended to exploit any gaps in the enemy line.

light tank: A tank that is built for speed rather than simply for protection.

The FT was the first tank to have a fully rotating turret. This set the pattern for all future tanks.

An American FT drives past infantrymen on its way to the front.

MODEL FOR THE FUTURE

What made the Renault different was its rotating turret, which housed a single gun. The tank had the engine in back, the driver at the front, and the turret on top. This would become standard for all tank design. The tank was tested in early 1917 and was an instant success. It was short, making it hard to cross trenches, but its large front wheel meant it could climb steep obstacles easily. It was first used in combat on May 31, 1918, in the effort to stop the German Spring Offensive.

BEE SWARM

The FT was cheap to build: it cost about one-fifth of the price of a **heavy tank**. About 3,000 were produced, and both the French and U.S. armies used the tank in the final months of the war. The French wanted to use the FT as a "bee swarm" to swamp German positions.

heavy tank: A slow tank with heavy armor and a powerful gun.

Recruits of the Lincolnshire Regiment in Britain practice rifle **drill** in September 1914, soon after the start of the war.

Rifle

Almost all infantrymen in World War I carried a **bolt-action** rifle, so called because a groove inside the barrel made bullets spin. This made the rifles very accurate compared with previous smoothbore, or ungrooved, weapons. Rifles were efficient, and they underwent few improvements during the conflict. Practice in using a rifle was the most important part of an infantryman's training.

bolt-action: A weapon loaded through a chamber at the rear end of the barrel.

An American infantryman drills using his Springfield Model 1903, the standard U.S. rifle of World War I.

EFFICIENT FIRING

The rifle's efficiency depended on the skill of its user. The rifleman drilled to push every round into his rifle and then eject the used cartridge case. The best riflemen could fire up to 15 rounds a minute. The maximum range of a rifle was 3,500 yards (3,200 m), but the weapons were inaccurate at distances above 600 yards (548 m).

British soldiers were issued the Lee-Enfield rifle, which was probably the most reliable rifle of the war. After 1917, U.S. General John Pershing was determined that his soldiers would use their rifles before any other weapon. He ordered that nothing should interfere with their rifle practice.

EYEWITNESS

"You must not forget that the rifle is distinctively an American weapon. I want to see it employed."

John Pershing
General, U.S. Army

drill: To practice a series of movements so that they become automatic when under fire.

A range of trench mortars. The flat support was necessary to absorb the recoil as the weapon fired.

Stokes Mortar

When trench lines extended across the Western Front after 1914, both sides realized that they needed a weapon that could be fired from the safety of a trench to fall into the enemy's trenches. This weapon would need to launch a projectile at an angle of over 45 degrees. The solution was a type of weapon that had fallen into disuse: the mortar.

mortar: A gun with a short, stubby barrel and a high angle of firing.

THE STOKES MORTAR

In January 1915, Sir Wilfred Stokes designed a lightweight mortar that became standard issue for British and Commonwealth armies. The device was a smooth metal tube with a firing pin at its base. It could fire 22 bombs a minute with a range of 1,200 yards (1,100 m).

The bombs weighed around 10 pounds (4.5 kg) and measured 3 inches (7.6 cm). The **safety pin** was removed as the bomb was dropped into the tube. The firing lever then sent the bomb high into the sky. It landed with a distinctive "plop" before detonating.

EYEWITNESS

"On one occasion a ham-fisted operator pulled out the safety pin and let the firing lever loose before the projectile entered the barrel. The cartridge misfired and we leaped from the trench just before the mortar exploded."

Sir Hugh Chance
Worcestershire Regiment

A British operator removes the safety pin as he drops a shell into a Stokes mortar on the Western Front in France in 1917.

A British crew in the Middle East prepares to fire a Stokes mortar from behind a wall of sandbags.

safety pin: A device that ensures that a firearm cannot go off accidentally.

Tank

Moving across a battlefield when deadly machine gun bullets were flying through the air was a problem for all armies engaged in World War I. The problem was made even worse on the Western Front because of the mud and obstacles there. The British answer was a weapon code-named "tank" to make the Germans think it was a water tank; the name stuck. The British government quickly ordered 100 of the lumbering monsters.

The British Mark IV tank had a crew of eight. It was armed with either 6-pounder (3 kg) guns or machine guns. Its **armor** was over ¼ inch (6 mm) thick.

armor: A protective covering against enemy weapons.

British infantry ride on a Mark IV tank. The caterpillar tracks allowed the vehicle to overcome obstacles on the battlefield.

CATERPILLAR TRACKS

The tank's key innovation was its **caterpillar tracks**. They allowed it to cross any terrain, although it moved only at about 5 miles per hour (7 km/h). The tanks were armed with a combination of naval 6-pounder (3 kg) guns and machine guns.

The British Mark I first appeared at the Battle of the Somme on September 15, 1916. Of the 49 tanks used, only 18 reached the enemy trenches. The rest broke down or got stuck. Even so, their impact was terrifying. A new weapon had been born.

EYEWITNESS

"Just before zero hour...these tanks appeared...We didn't know what they were because we hadn't heard anything about them. It was an amazing sight."

Edward Gale
Corporal, British Army,
Battle of the Somme

caterpillar tracks: Tracks made of a continuous band of joined metal platelets.

Torpedo

Torpedoes had been developed in the late 19th century as missiles that could be fired from small torpedo boats to damage battleships. During World War I, torpedoes were usually powered by propellers driven by compressed air. They could be dropped from aircraft or fired from surface vessels, but their main use was by submarines.

A British Sopwith T1 flies low over the ocean as it releases a torpedo. Torpedoes could be fired from aircraft, submarines, or surface ships.

compressed air: Air that is kept under pressure so it can be used as a propellant.

A ship blows up as a torpedo strikes it amidships. Torpedoes were designed to strike on or just below the waterline.

SINKING THE *LUSITANIA*

In World War I, German U-boats (*Unterseeboots*, or submarines) used torpedoes to sink merchant ships in the Atlantic. They also surfaced to attack unarmed vessels with their machine guns. Among the U-boats' victims was the *Lusitania*, a U.S. passenger liner. The ship's sinking caused the United States to declare war on Germany in 1917.

The Allies fought back by firing torpedoes from their own submarines or from torpedo boats. They dropped torpedoes and bombs from new aircraft like the Short Bomber. They also laid large fields of mines, or floating bombs. Eventually the Allies sank so many U-boats that the threat largely disappeared.

EYEWITNESS

"There was a fountain of water, a burst of smoke, a flash of fire, and part of the cruiser rose in the air. Then I heard a roar and felt reverberations through the water by the detonations. [The ship] had broken apart, and sank in a few minutes."

Otto Weddigen
Commander, *U-9*, 1916

amidships: A naval word meaning the middle of a ship.

A replica Sopwith triplane banks into a turn. The triplane was easier to maneuver than most biplanes, and the pilot could see more easily.

Triplane

After the development of the forward-firing machine gun in airplanes, both sides raced to create the best fighting aircraft. For a time in 1917 and 1918, the best technology seemed to be the triplane. A triplane gave the pilot a better view. The extra wing also allowed the plane to be narrower, which gave it extra **lift** and made it more maneuverable. A red Fokker triplane was the plane flown by the most famous fighter pilot of the war, Manfred von Richtofen, the "Red Baron."

lift: The force that makes an airplane take off when air passes quickly over the wing.

SOPWITH TRIPLANE

The British-designed Sopwith triplane was produced in less than three months. Its test flight in May 1916 went so well that it was sent to the front line soon after. The triplanes could climb 5,000 feet (1,524 m) in four and a half minutes and reached an unheard-of **elevation** of 20,000 feet (6,100 m).

EYEWITNESS

"By now the German triplane was in the middle of our formation, and its handling was wonderful to behold. The pilot seemed to be firing at all of us simultaneously."

James McCudden
British flight commander

So many Allied pilots had died in "Bloody April" 1916 that their average life expectancy was just 11 days. The Sopwith helped balance the fight. It was also flown by the famous all-Canadian Black Flight. The German command demanded its own triplanes. The most successful was the Fokker. Triplanes often proved unreliable, however. That meant their popularity was over by the middle of 1918.

The Armstrong-Whitworth FK12 was a triplane gunship produced by the British in 1916.

elevation: The distance of something above the ground.

Glossary

automatic: A weapon that continues to fire until the trigger is released.

battery: A group of artillery weapons that operate together as one unit.

blockade: To use ships to prevent a country from importing or exporting supplies.

broadside: When all the guns on one side of a ship fire at the same time.

chlorine: A chemical that, as a gas, can irritate the lungs and cause suffocation and death.

close-quarter: Hand-to-hand fighting with an enemy who is within touching distance.

counterattack: To attack the enemy after they have attacked you.

dug in: Protected in strong defensive positions, with trenches and other barriers.

fuse: A mechanical or electrical device for detonating the explosives in a bomb.

limber: A two-wheeled vehicle that can carry a gun or a container of ammunition.

mortar: A gun with a short, stubby barrel and a high angle of firing.

no-man's land: The land lying between the two enemy trenches on the Western Front.

over the top: The name for the moment soldiers leave their trenches to begin an advance.

pistols: Small handguns often carried by officers, pilots, and other soldiers.

recoil: The kickback of a gun when it is fired.

reconnaissance: Gathering information about enemy positions.

round: The military name for a single shot fired by a weapon.

semiautomatic: A weapon that fires repeatedly when the trigger is pressed.

shrapnel: Fragments of metal that fly out of an exploding shell.

stalemate: A point at which neither side can gain an advantage over the other.

trajectory: The path of a flying object from when it is launched until it lands.

trenches: Defensive positions that were dug into the ground.

turret: A revolving structure placed on top of a vehicle or ship, usually to house a gun.

Further Information

Cornish, Paul. *Machine Guns and the Great War.* Pen and Sword, 2021.

Doeden, Matt. *Weapons of World War I.* Capstone Press, 2017.

Friedman, Norman. *Naval Weapons of World War I.* Seaforth Publishing, 2021.

Neiberg, Michael S. *World War I Illustrated Atlas.* Amber Books, 2022.

Smithsonian. *World War I: The Definitive Visual History.* Dorling Kindersley, 2018.

Ward, Edward and Ronny Bar. *German Aircraft of World War I.* Amber Books, 2022.

Zaloga, Stephen J. and Felipe Rodriguez. *The French 75.* Osprey Publishing, 2020.

Websites

https://www.studentsofhistory.com/new-weapons-ww1
This site gives an overview of advances in weapons technology during World War I.

https://alphahistory.com/worldwar1/weapons/htm
Read a brief overview of the various types of weapons used in land warfare during World War I.

https://www.theworldwar.org
This site contains a large collection of information about World War I and the weapons used in the conflict. It includes informative videos.

https://www.firstworldwar.com/weaponry
Take a look at the main weapons used in trenches on the Western Front.

Publisher's note to educators and parents: Our editors have carefully reviewed these websites to ensure that they are suitable for students. Many websites change frequently, however, and we cannot guarantee that a site's future contents will continue to meet our high standards of quality and educational value. Be advised that students should be closely supervised whenever they access the Internet.

Index